SIR WALTER SCOTT
from a painting by ANDREW GEDDES
Scottish National Portrait Gallery

SIR WALTER SCOTT

by
IAN JACK

PUBLISHED FOR
THE BRITISH COUNCIL
BY LONGMAN GROUP LTD

LONGMAN GROUP LTD
Longman House, Burnt Mill, Harlow, Essex

*Associated companies, branches and
representatives throughout the world*

First published 1958
Reprinted with additions to Bibliography 1964, 1971
© Ian Jack, 1958, 1971

*Printed in Great Britain by
F. Mildner & Sons, London, EC1R 5EJ*

SBN 0 582 01103 5

SIR WALTER SCOTT

TWENTY-FIVE years ago Edmund Wilson remarked on the anomalous place occupied by Dickens among the great English writers. He pointed out that while Dickens had come to be taken for granted as an institution, his true stature as a writer was not appreciated. Today the position of Dickens is very different, and there are signs that it is Scott who has fallen heir to this prominent but neglected niche in the Temple of Fame. He too enjoys—if that is the word—the sort of household familiarity that has nothing much to do with being read. It is as true of Scott today as it was of Dickens yesterday that 'the literary men from Oxford and Cambridge . . . rather snubbingly leave him alone', and while a good deal has recently been written about him—notably by Grierson and his distinguished successors as Scott Lecturer in the University of Edinburgh —there is still no comprehensive modern biography, no incisive critical survey. The most stimulating writers on the novel have tended to ignore Scott or refer to him with an unbecoming condescension. The scholars have been more industrious, but they have not done enough. No wholly reliable edition of the novels exists. No edition of Lockhart's *Life* corresponding to the Hill-Powell edition of Boswell has yet been produced. Grierson's book, 'Supplementary to, and Corrective of, Lockhart's Biography', has many merits; but it does not stand very satisfactorily on its own feet. The prevailing half-heartedness about Scott is oddly summed up by the fact that while his letters have at last been collected, no index has yet been published, so that the wealth of information about the man himself and the literary history of his time contained in these twelve volumes remains almost as inaccessible as it was before.

It is not difficult to account for this state of affairs. The unevenness of Scott's work is notorious, and no service is done to his memory by enthusiasts who find *Woodstock* as

rewarding as *The Heart of Mid-Lothian* and persist in pre-
scribing *Ivanhoe* as a 'set book'. The casualness with which
Scott approached his literary undertakings, whether we
regard it as a splendid magnanimity or a culpable indifference
to his art, is calculated to make scholars feel small and
ridiculous. He was not greatly concerned with the theory
of fiction, and his books contain less to interest critics
writing on the evolution of the modern novel than the
work of many much less gifted men. And then there is
Lockhart. His biography, admirable as it is, is not of a sort
to give us much sense of kinship with its subject. Precisely
because Scott was so fine a person—so much of the man as
well as the gentleman—we need a biography which should
acknowledge such faults as he had. What his biographer
gives us is a carefully-edited Scott. We know now that the
story of Scott on his death-bed telling Lockhart to be a good
man may well be a fabrication, and we are on our guard.
Remembering Lockhart's disingenuous career as a reviewer,
we do not trust him. It is not so much that details here and
there are faked: the scholars who know most about Scott
assure us that there are not many of these. It is rather that the
whole thing is too deliberately posed, too much of an
Academy portrait. Scott was one of Raeburn's favourite
subjects, as Johnson was of Reynolds, and the difference
between Boswell's biography and Lockhart's is precisely
that between the portraits of these two painters. Boswell
presents Johnson as Reynolds painted him: massive,
impressive, uncouth, unmistakably true: Lockhart's Scott is
Raeburn's Scott: nobly conceived, yet painted with a senti-
mentality that softens the outlines and detracts somehow
from the reality of the sitter. The result is a figure curiously
remote from the lives of most of us. It is hardly surprising
that a critic as gifted as Edwin Muir has been driven, as if
in sheer desperation, to formulate a psychological theory to
explain some of the surprising features of Scott as a man and
as a writer: an unconvincing theory that may be regarded
less as an attempt to pull Scott down from his pedestal than

as an endeavour to confer on him a common humanity with ourselves.

There is something to be said for by-passing Lockhart, and fortunately we can go straight to Scott himself. Although he was one of the least introspective of authors, hardly any prose-writer before Henry James wrote so much about his own life and the composition of his books. In his late thirties, before he had published a single novel, he wrote a chapter of autobiography about twice the length of this essay in which he tells us precisely the things about his early life that we are most anxious to know. Throughout his life he was as voluminous a letter-writer as any of the Victorians. In his later years he kept a Journal in which we are admitted—or as nearly admitted as he was willing or able to admit anyone—to his private thoughts; while the prefaces which he wrote for the collected edition of his writings form a series of chapters of literary autobiography which take up the story about the point where his autobiography proper had left it, and bring us within sight of the end.

II

Scott points out in his autobiography that every Scotsman has a pedigree, and he himself took great pleasure in tracing his descent through his great-grandfather, a Jacobite 'well-known in Teviotdale by the name of Beardie', back to Auld Watt of Harden and beyond, liking to think of his remoter ancestors as 'merrymen all, of the persuasion and calling of Robin Hood and Little John'. His immediate origins were very different, his father being an Edinburgh solicitor, a Writer to the Signet; he was an unworldly man, a strict Calvinist and an enthusiastic student of theology and of 'the abstruse feudal doctrines connected with conveyancing'. Scott's mother, a woman of pronounced literary tastes, was the eldest daughter of a highly gifted

Professor of Medicine at the University. The contrast between the uneventful respectability of his early surroundings and what he conceived of as the romance of his remoter ancestry, which was to be the mainspring of so much of his writing seems to have struck Scott at an early age. Crippled by paralysis in his infancy, he was as a child a great listener to the tales of his elders. He loved to listen to his uncle Thomas Scott, for example, and comments that 'it was a fine thing to hear him talk over the change in the country which he had witnessed'. There was also his grandmother, 'in whose youth the old Border depredations were matters of recent tradition, [and who] used to tell me many a tale of Watt of Harden, Wight Willie of Aikwood, Jamie Telfer of the fair Dodhead, and other heroes'. And there was George Constable, on whom the Antiquary is partly modelled, who remembered the rebellion of 1745 and liked to talk about 'subjects of history or auldlangsyne'. Edinburgh is a highly antiquarian city, and few men are so apt to be antiquarians as elderly Writers to the Signet. It was Scott's good fortune as a boy to be surrounded by a sort of Greek Chorus of Scots Antiquaries, with the retentive memory and the love of moralizing characteristic of their classical counterparts, but with a satirical sense of humour super-added.

It is clear that the stories and traditions which he heard from his elders were the material of Scott's earliest daydreams. Like Waverley, he 'would steal away to indulge the fancies they excited. In the corner of a large and sombre library . . . he would exercise for hours that internal sorcery, as it were, to the eye of the muser'. What he heard by which past or imaginary events are presented in action, was soon supplemented by what he read. Classical literature made little appeal to him, but he read widely in the English poets, particularly those who 'exercised themselves on romantic fiction'. He was fond of historical works, and read 'many picturesque and interesting passages from our old historical chronicles'. Later he began to explore Italian and French literature in a random way. He was particularly struck by 'the heart-stirring and eye-dazzling descriptions of war and of tournaments' in Froissart, as well as by the historical works of Brantôme and de la Noue, from whom he 'learned to compare the wild and loose and yet superstitious character of the nobles of the League, with the stern, rigid, and sometimes turbulent disposition of the Huguenot party'—a comparison that he must have remembered when he came to contrast Jacobite and Hanoverian, Highlander and Lowlander, Royalist and Roundhead, in his own books.

But that is to anticipate. From his earliest boyhood Scott loved to hear traditional songs, particularly those associated with Border raids or the adventures of the Jacobites. He had a remarkable facility in learning them by heart, and would interrupt visitors anxious to talk with his elders by shouting dozens of stanzas of the ballad of Hardicanute at the top of his voice: 'one may as well speak in the mouth of a cannon as where that child is', as one of them complained. When therefore he came on Allan Ramsay's *Tea-Table Miscellany* and a little later Percy's *Reliques of Ancient English Poetry*, he was enchanted. 'As I had been from infancy devoted to legendary lore of this nature', he comments, 'it may be imagined . . . with what delight I saw pieces of the same kind which had amused my childhood, and still continued in secret the Delilahs of my imagination, considered as the subjects of sober research.' Though he never lost his limp, his health became in every other respect extremely robust, and he tells us that as a young man he would often walk thirty miles in a day, or ride a hundred. On these expeditions he was in the habit of persuading the old men and women who knew traditional songs and ballads to recite them for him (though how often he wrote these down himself, as distinct from begging written copies from his fellow-enthusiasts, remains obscure). At first he was discouraged from publishing his collection 'by the multitude of similar publications', but finally he decided to try his fortune, and the result was the *Minstrelsy of the Scottish Border*, of which the first two volumes were published in 1802 and the third the following year. He regarded the 'Raiding Ballads (as they are called) relating to the forays and predatory incursions made upon the Borders' as a special feature of his collection, but he also included ballads of other types as well as modern imitations. Like Percy he wanted to reach as wide an audience as possible, and did not hesitate to complete unfinished ballads or improve passages which he regarded as unsatisfactory. He did the same with *Sir Tristrem*, a poem commonly attributed to Thomas the Rhymer, which he published in 1804 provided with a brief final 'fytte' of his own composition.

The transition from this sort of editing to original composition was a very easy one, and although Scott was for a while fascinated by some modish German poetry—his first publication was entitled *The Chase, and William and Helen: two ballads from the German of Burger*—his most important inspiration as a poet came to him from the traditional poetry of Scotland. When he determined to attempt a longer poem his first desire was to write something in the ballad-stanza, while for a subject he wanted a story 'which might admit of being treated with the simplicity and wildness of an ancient ballad'. Chance provided him with the story of the dwarf Gilpin Horner; and though he realized that a long poem in the ballad-stanza would not be popular, he was able to evolve a metrical form which owed as much to traditional poetry as to the experiments of his contemporaries. Impressed by the metrical experiments of Southey and by Coleridge's *Christabel*, he used a medley of metres which provided him with splendid opportunities for the effects of contrast of which he was so fond, yet in which the tetrameter couplet 'so popular with our old minstrels' remained in the background as a sort of norm. His poetry has something in common with that of the Italian *improvisatori*: it is swift-moving verse in which eloquent passages alternate with others which are culpably careless, and yet which carries us on and on as if we were caught up by some powerful and irresistible current.

The historical and antiquarian interests which are so evident in the *Minstrelsy* are no less characteristic of Scott's original poems. *The Lay of the Last Minstrel* is 'intended to illustrate the customs and manners which anciently prevailed on the Borders of England and Scotland'. Scott recognized that the Borderers of the sixteenth century, 'living in a state partly pastoral, and partly warlike, and combining habits of constant depredation with the influence of a rude spirit of chivalry, provided a subject peculiarly adapted to poetry'. *Marmion* is 'an attempt to paint the manners of the feudal times upon a broader scale', while *The Lady of the Lake* is introduced by the remark that 'the ancient manners . . . of the aboriginal race by whom the Highlands of Scotland were inhabited, had always appeared to me peculiarly adapted to poetry'.

Like the poetry of Rogers and Campbell, and indeed the first two Cantos of *Childe Harold's Pilgrimage*, Scott's long poems enjoyed a popularity in their own day which they will never recover. Written to suit the taste of the age, to provide the common reader with a first-rate pastime, they lack the seriousness of major poetry. While the modern reader is still struck by the vigour of the verse and the boyish zest with which Scott describes his feuds and battles and pursuits, he may be impressed more deeply by a certain underlying sadness, as he reads:

> Of ancient deeds, so long forgot;
> Of feuds, whose memory was not;
> Of forests now laid waste and bare;
> Of towers, which harbour now the hare;
> Of manners, long since changed and gone.

It is when Scott touches on the oldest of all poetic themes, the transitoriness of human life, that he comes nearest to memorable eloquence:

> Now is the stately column broke,
> The beacon-light is quenched in smoke,
> The trumpet's silver sound is still,
> The warder silent on the hill.

There are two or three lyrics in *Waverley* and its successors which remain haunting the memory when *Marmion* has been forgotten: 'Proud Maisie' in *The Heart of Mid-Lothian*, for example, or these lines from *The Bride of Lammermoor*:

> Look not thou on beauty's charming,
> Sit thou still when kings are arming,
> Taste not when the wine-cup glistens,
> Speak not when the people listens,
> Stop thine ear against the singer,
> From the red gold keep thy finger;
> Vacant heart and hand and eye,
> Easy live and quiet die.

III

When we turn from the poems to *Waverley* and its successors we turn from romances in verse to romances in prose. Scott tells us that he called his poems 'romances' 'because the description of scenery and manners was more the object of the Author than a combined and regular narrative'. Although his practice was not consistent, he more often used the word 'romance' than 'novel' to describe his works of prose fiction, and the introductory epistle to *The Fortunes of Nigel* makes it clear that he recoiled from the labour of writing a novel with a regular plot 'where every step brings us a point nearer to the final catastrophe' precisely as he recoiled from the task of writing a 'regular' poem.

As many critics have noticed, in most of Scott's books elements of the romance may be found combined with elements of the novel. But what precisely is meant by the two terms? A romance is written simply to entertain. It is not a serious criticism of life, and is not tied to the rules of probability. Its characterization is likely to be superficial—particularly the characterization of the hero and heroine—and it will probably describe exciting events, 'moving accidents by flood and field'. The setting may be romantic and unfamiliar, giving the author opportunities for picturesque description. There is often an element of wish-fulfilment, the reader being encouraged to identify himself with the hero or heroine. The novel, on the other hand, does aim at a criticism of life: its function is to entertain, but to do so by telling the truth about human existence. For this reason it is tied more or less strictly to the laws of probability, and satire may be prominent. The setting may well be that of the author's own daily life, the incidents such as might happen to anyone. The characterization of one or two central figures will tend to be all-important: dialogue will matter more than description. In the work of most of the English novelists there is something of both elements, though sometimes the romance is more prominent and sometimes the novel. In *Emma*, for example, there is a great deal of the novel, very little of the romance. In *Wuthering Heights* the element of the romance is much more prominent. It is interesting to remember that the work of Mrs Radcliffe and her followers, satirized by Jane Austen, must have helped to nourish the strange creative genius of the Brontës. Scott resembled the Brontës (who were to be eager readers of his books) in being attracted by the remote, the mysterious, the picturesque.

From his boyhood onwards he was a story-teller. When he was at school he had a close friend called John Irving, and he tells us that they had an agreement by which each in turn would 'compose a romance for the other's amusement'. He was in no doubt about the importance of this early habit:

These legends, in which the martial and the miraculous always predominated, we rehearsed to each other during our walks. . . . Whole holidays were spent in this singular pastime, which continued for two or three years, and had, I believe, no small effect in directing the turn of my imagination to the chivalrous and romantic in poetry and prose.

The first story in prose that we know Scott to have begun with the intention of publication was the offspring of these early romances. It was to be 'a tale of chivalry . . . in the style of *The Castle of Otranto*, with plenty of Border characters and supernatural incident', and the part that was written was included as an appendix to the later editions of *Waverley*. Two other fragments written before the publication of *Waverley*—of which the first third was composed in 1805 and then thrown aside—are given in other appendices, and each anticipates a direction which Scott was later to pursue more fully. One was set in Scotland in the seventeenth and eighteenth centuries and was to be called *The Lord of Ennerdale*. The other was a brief conclusion for a romance written by the antiquary Joseph Strutt; its scene was laid in the reign of Henry VI, and the intention was 'to illustrate the manners, customs, and language of the people of England during that period'. The failure of Strutt's book, *Queenhoo-Hall*, drove Scott to the conclusion that 'the manners of the middle ages did not possess the interest which [he] had conceived'.

While the modern reader is more likely to recognize the element of the romance in Scott's later books it is important to realize that he himself also thought of *Waverley* as falling into this category: he called it 'a romance, founded on a Highland story, and more modern events' than *Queenhoo-Hall*, and considered that such a book 'would have a better chance of popularity than a tale of chivalry'. After his famous journey to the Highlands and Islands in 1773, Samuel Johnson had half rejoiced and half complained that 'such is the effect of the late regulations, that a longer journey than to the Highlands must be taken by him whose curiosity pants for savage virtues and barbarous grandeur'. By travelling backwards in time Scott was able to make this 'longer journey'. When Rose Bradwardine gave Waverley an account of a Highland feud, we are told, he

> could not help starting at a story which bore so much resemblance to one of his own day-dreams. Here was a girl . . . who had witnessed with her own eyes such a scene as he had used to conjure up in his imagination, as only occurring in ancient times . . . He might have said with Malvolio, ' "I do not now fool myself, to let imagination jade me", I am actually in the land of military and romantic adventures.'

Scott had found in Scotland's past people and events as romantic as anything that he had discovered in imaginative literature. His aim in the Scotch Novels (as they were originally called) was to communicate his imaginative excitement to his readers.

This intention explains the structure of *Waverley, or, 'Tis Sixty Years Since*. As Jeffrey pointed out, all that really happens in the first half of the book is that the hero travels into Scotland and learns about 'the manners and state of society that prevailed . . . in the earlier part of last century'. Such chapter-headings as 'A Horse-Quarter in Scotland', 'A Scottish Manor-House Sixty Years Since', and 'A Creagh[1] and its Consequences' tell their own story. Since Waverley travels on behalf of the reader, everything is made easy for him; we are hardly surprised when the famous robber Evan Dhu invites him to study the methods of the cattle-thieves at first hand. The people whom Waverley meets are as carefully chosen as those selected to be introduced to a royal personage: they are the best possible examples of a characteristic type. Baron Bradwardine, for example, is 'the very model of the old Scottish cavalier . . . a character . . . which is fast disappearing'. When Waverley returns to the Lowlands, later in the book, he is just as privileged a spectator: he blunders into the '45, attends the Jacobite Ball at Holyrood, meets the Chevalier, and witnesses the Battle of Preston.

Waverley's journey into Scotland and into a past more romantic than the present was to be taken by tens of

[1] raid.

thousands of readers in the years that followed. The six books that succeeded it all describe Scotland in the eighteenth century or at the end of the seventeenth, and this was Scott's true area of inspiration. When in *Ivanhoe* and many of the later romances he turned to other settings, he ceased to be a major writer. But what matters is a man's best work, and Scott's genius must be estimated by the series of books that ended with *The Heart of Mid-Lothian*, supplemented by those of the later volumes—such as *Redgauntlet*—in which he returned to the life which he fully understood.

IV

Scott was delighted with the reception given to *Waverley*, and it is clear that he determined to follow it with a book exploiting the same rich vein yet free from the glaring deficiencies of his first attempt. While the central purpose of *Guy Mannering* is again to illustrate Scottish life at a certain period—in the last quarter of the eighteenth century —and while its hero is again an Englishman coming to Scotland for the first time, it improves on its model in at least three ways. Although it is not a masterpiece of construction, its plot is much superior to that of the first book. Secondly, while men and women characteristic of the period are the main actors, historical personages and events are avoided, so that it is a 'historical romance' in a different sense. But what is most important is that *Guy Mannering* contains a number of the remarkable characters whose speeches form the element of greatness in all his best work. Dandie Dinmont, who is based on a type that Scott knew well, is a notable achievement. His speech on the education of dogs—'Beast or body, education should aye be minded'—is in itself better than anything in *Waverley*. Meg Merrilees is of particular significance. Scott had always been attracted by gypsies, as he was by any class of people who lived according to an older and freer code than that of his contemporaries; he refers to them as 'the *Parias* of Scotland, living like wild Indians among European settlers, and, like them, judged of rather by their own customs, habits, and opinions, than as if they had been members of the civilized part of the community'. Meg is not only the lynch-pin of the whole action: she also acts as a remarkably impressive chorus. Here is the curse that she pronounces when her tribe is turned away from the land where they had long been suffered to remain:

Ride your ways, ride your ways, Laird of Ellangowan—ride your ways, Godfrey Bertram!—This day have ye quenched seven smoking hearths —see if the fire in your ain parlour burn the blyther for that. Ye have riven the thack of seven cottar houses—look if your ain roof-tree stand the faster.—Ye may stable your stirks in the shealings at Derncleugh—see that the hare does not couch on the hearthstone at Ellangowan.—Ride your ways, Godfrey Bertram—what do you glower after our folk for? There's thirty hearts there, that wad hae wanted bread ere ye had wanted sunkets, and spent their lifeblood ere ye had scratched your finger. Yes, there's thirty yonder, from the auld wife of an hundred to the babe that was born last week, that ye have turned out o' their bits o' bields, to sleep with the tod and the blackcock in the muirs!—Ride your ways, Ellangowan.—Our bairns are hinging at our weary backs—look that your braw cradle at hame be the fairer spread up.[1]

This speech emphasized the theme which runs through the whole book. *Guy Mannering* is a study in loyalties, a study in the changes that had come over Scotland. Harlot and thief as she is, Meg Merrilees recognizes ancient ties to which the 'new men', and even the younger gypsies, are strangers. She is a sort of picturesque reincarnation of the Last Minstrel, lamenting the changes that have befallen Scotland as the feudal order has been hurried towards its end.

Edie Ochiltree's role in *The Antiquary* is in many ways analogous, but the spirit of comedy is prominent in this third of the *Waverleys* (set during the years when Scott was

---

[1] thack, thatch; shealings, sheds, cottages; sunkets, delicacies; bits o' bields, poor shelters; tod, fox.

a young man) and his first appearance is one of the great comic moments in fiction. The Antiquary is explaining to the hero how he has discovered the remains of a Roman camp which will at last settle the question of the site of the battle of Mons Graupius:

'Yes, my dear friend, from this stance it is probably—nay, it is nearly certain, that Julius Agricola beheld what our Beaumont has so admirably described!—From this very Praetorium—'

A voice from behind interrupted this ecstatic description—'Praetorian here, Praetorian there, I mind the bigging o't'.[1]

Edie Ochiltree, the wandering beggar 'who kept his rounds within a particular space, and was the newscarrier, the minstrel, and sometimes the historian of the district, [a] rascal [who] knows more old ballads and traditions than any other man in this, and the next four parishes', is another example of the type of character that made the deepest appeal to Scott, and inspired his greatest speeches:

I have had many a thought, that when I faund mysell auld and forfairn, and no able to enjoy God's blessed air ony langer, I wad drag mysell here wi'a pickle aitmeal ... and I wad e'en streek mysell out here, and abide my removal, like an auld dog that trails his useless ugsome carcase into some bush or bracken, no to gie living things a scunner wi' the sight o't when it's dead—Ay, and then, when the dogs barked at the lone farm-stead, the gudewife wad cry, 'Whisht, sirra, that'll be auld Edie', and the bits o' weans wad up, puir things, and toddle to the door, to pu' in the auld Blue Gown that mends a' their bonny-dies—but there wad be nae mair word o' Edie, I trow.[2]

Edie's speeches are not the only examples of Scott's triumphant use of the Lowland vernacular in this book. One of the most Wordsworthian things in it occurs during the description of the funeral near the end:

[1] I remember its being built.

[2] forfairn, worn out; pickle, small supply of; streek mysell, lay myself out (like a corpse); ugsome, disgusting; scunner, disgust; bits o' weans, little children; bonny-dies, toys.

'I'm fain to see ye looking sae weel, cummer; the mair, that the black ox
has tramped on ye since I was aneath your roof-tree.'

'Ay,' said Elspeth; but rather from a general idea of misfortune, than
any exact recollection of what had happened—'there has been distress
amang us of late—I wonder how younger folk bide it—I bide it ill—I
canna hear the wind whistle, and the sea roar, but I think I see the coble
whombled keel up, and some o' them struggling in the waves—Eh, sirs,
sic weary dreams as folk hae between sleeping and waking, before they
win to the lang sleep and the sound.'[1]

By the time when he wrote *The Antiquary* Scott was
perfectly aware that the great strength of his writing lay
in his creation of Scots character through his use of the Scots
tongue. He points out in the preface that he has sought his
principal characters

in the class of society who are the last to feel the influence of that general
polish which assimilates to each other the manners of different nations
. . . both because the lower orders are less restrained by the habit of
suppressing their feelings, and because I agree with my friend Words-
worth that they seldom fail to express them in the strongest and most
powerful language. This is, I think, peculiarly the case with the peasantry
of my own country, a class with whom I have long been familiar. The
antique force and simplicity of their language, often tinctured with the
Oriental eloquence of Scripture . . . give pathos to their grief and dignity
to their resentment.

We again find speeches of this sort in *Old Mortality*, the
first book in which Scott wrote of a period about which his
information was derived wholly from written sources; and
we find them, most notably of all, in *The Heart of Mid-
Lothian*, a remarkable work which must be regarded as the
one great masterpiece of the *Waverley* series. In this book, for
the first time, there is no upper-class hero or heroine. The
central character, Jeanie Deans, speaks Scots. In *Rob Roy*
Scott was to show his boredom with the usual heroine of
romance by creating the tomboy Di Vernon; but Jeanie
Deans differs from convention much more profoundly.

[1] fain, glad; cummer, gossip, neighbour; the black ox, death; bide,
stand; coble, cobble, small boat; whombled, overturned.

The book was written to demonstrate 'the possibility of rendering a fictitious personage interesting by mere dignity of mind and rectitude of principle, assisted by unpretending good sense and temper, without any of the beauty, grace, talent, accomplishment, and wit, to which a heroine of romance is supposed to have a prescriptive right'. Jeanie Deans is in fact no more 'born to be an heroine' than Catherine Morland in *Northanger Abbey*. It is characteristic that when the Duke of Argyle carries her off and 'a romantic heroine might have suspected and dreaded the power of her own charms', no such 'silly thought' presents itself to her mind. Jeanie Deans has graver issues to deal with than those confronting the heroines of romance. What is at stake is her integrity of conscience. Time and again the great temptation is pressed on her: if only she will affirm that her sister had told her that she was pregnant, she will save her life: and she knows that her sister is innocent of the child-murder of which she is suspected. In this dilemma her determination is simple and unshakeable: for her sister she will sacrifice 'all but truth and conscience'. In analyzing her response to a potentially tragic situation Scott shows his understanding of the Lowland Scots character, as the product of environment and history, at a level far transcending the merely curious or picturesque. Jeanie Deans's journey southwards to plead for her sister's life contrasts markedly with the journey northwards undertaken by so many of his heroes. This is a serious journey, undertaken as a quest for justice and mercy, an expedition closer to Bunyan than to the guide-book. In the story as it came to Scott—in an anonymous letter written by a Mrs Helen Goldie—it was the Duke of Argyle who procured the pardon. Scott enhances the drama by introducing the Porteous Riots as the background of the story—and so emphasizing the theme of confusion and uncertainty about human justice—and by making Jeanie herself plead for her sister's life before the Queen. The words in which she does so have the resonance of the greatest human utterances:

O, madam, if ever ye kend what it was to sorrow for and with a sinning and a suffering creature, whose mind is sae tossed that she can be neither ca'd fit to live or die, have some compassion on our misery! Save an honest house from dishonour, and an unhappy girl, not eighteen years of age, from an early and dreadful death! Alas! it is not when we sleep soft and wake merrily ourselves that we think on other people's sufferings. Our hearts are waxed light within us then, and we are for righting our ain wrangs and fighting our ain battles. But when the hour of trouble comes to the mind or to the body—and seldom may it visit your Leddy-ship—and when the hour of death comes, that comes to high and low—lang, and late may it be yours—O, my Leddy, then it isna what we hae dune for oursells, but what we hae dune for others, that we think on most pleasantly. And the thoughts that ye hae intervened to spare the puir thing's life will be sweeter in that hour, come when it may, than if a word of your mouth could hang the haill Porteous mob at the tail of ae tow.[1]

The man who wrote that speech might have done anything. And yet Scott did not hesitate to add several hundred pages to his masterpiece to bring it to a length which suited his publisher, adding a novelettish postscript to his greatest imaginative achievement. 'A rogue writes to tell me', he wrote in his Journal, 'rather of the latest, if the matter was of consequence—that he approves of the first three volumes of the *H. of Midlothian*, but totally condemns the fourth. However, an author should be reasonably well pleased when three fourths of his works are acceptable to the reader.' It is surely the oddest remark ever made by a great writer.

V

Yet it is typical of Scott. He shared Dr Johnson's view that 'no man but a blockhead ever wrote, except for money'. While he took a natural pleasure in exercising his gift of storytelling, from the first his principal object in writing was to make money, and in the end he had no other.

---

[1] kend, have known; tail of ae tow, end of one rope.

Literary fame did not mean much to him, nor was literary immortality often in his thoughts. In his heart he despised literary people, if they were not also something more: as he listened to their talk he must have felt the easy amusement of a millionaire who overhears a small shopkeeper boasting of his savings. This might suggest that Scott was an exceptionally well-balanced man; and so in most ways he was. Yet perhaps no one is wholly sane, and he had his own obsession. He was obsessed by the idea of founding a family. There are no more illuminating pages in Lockhart—and none in which he speaks more frankly—than those in which he analyses the motives which impelled Scott on his way. 'His original pride', he tells us, 'was to be an acknowledged member of one of the "honourable families" whose progenitors had been celebrated . . . for following . . . in blind obedience . . . the patriarchal leader; his first and last wordly ambition was to be himself the founder of a distinct branch; he desired to plant a lasting root, and dreamt not of personal fame, but of long distant generations rejoicing in the name of "Scott of Abbotsford". By this idea all his reveries—all his aspirations—all his plans and efforts, were overshadowed and controlled.' Abbotsford, the house which he purchased in 1811 and extended and elaborated almost until the end, mattered to him more than anything that he had ever written. This 'romance in stone' was the symbol of what he was trying to do, the mistress for whom he laboured longer than any knight of medieval legend and for whom he was to sacrifice life itself. This is not the place to trace his bewildering relations with his publishers, or to attempt any distribution of the blame. If you are not interested in money it is wiser not to aim at becoming rich. The trouble with Scott was that he had a mind above money, yet he wanted a great deal of it. So he wrote and wrote, and in the end money brought him down.

In the preface to *Ivanhoe* Scott acknowledges the dilemma which had faced him after the publication of *Rob Roy*. 'Scottish manners, Scottish dialect, and Scottish characters of note, being those with which the author was most intimately and familiarly acquainted, were the ground upon which he had hitherto relied. It was, however, obvious that this kind of interest must in the end occasion a degree of sameness and repetition.' The remarkable thing is that change of setting was the chief means of variety which occurred to Scott.

When Dickens sensed that the first impulse of his imaginative invention was flagging, he took stock of the position and made a sustained and remarkable effort to write on a new plan. With *Dombey and Son*, as Kathleen Tillotson has argued, he began the attempt to write novels 'founded on a theme, embodied in a relation between characters'. Scott's main resource was to move from country to country and from century to century. In the imaginary dialogue between the author and a critic prefaced to one of his last books, *The Surgeon's Daughter*, he admits that he would be delighted 'to light upon any topic to supply the place of the Highlands', a theme that is 'becoming a little exhausted'. His friend replies: 'Do with your Muse of Fiction . . . as many an honest man does with his sons in flesh and blood . . . Send her to India.' And so, twenty years before Martin Chuzzlewit was sent to America, Adam Hartley was despatched to India, and this was only one of the last of the destinations in space and time to which Scott's heroes had been sent packing. It is no surprise that the part of *The Surgeon's Daughter* which is set in Scotland— the greater part—is much more successful than the Indian episode. A writer can only deal satisfactorily with the life that he knows. In his *Life of Mrs Radcliffe* Scott had pointed out the inferiority of her first book, *The Castles of Athlin and Dunbayne*, to its successors, commenting that 'the scene is laid in Scotland during the Dark Ages, but without any attempt to trace either the peculiar manners or scenery of the country'. Even if Mrs Radcliffe had made the attempt it may be doubted whether her book would have been much improved: she had never been in Scotland, and she had never lived in the Middle Ages: however conscientiously she had studied the background, therefore, it would have remained book-knowledge. And book-knowledge, for a creative writer, remains half-knowledge.

Scott seems not to have realized how profoundly *The Heart of Mid-Lothian* differed even from his other books set in eighteenth-century Scotland. The reason must have been that he was not greatly interested in theory and technique. He did not give much thought (for example) to the possibility of varying the storyteller's point of view. The fictitious autobiographies of his contemporary John Galt—above all *The Provost*, that masterpiece of sustained dramatic irony —have a technical maturity to which he did not aspire. 'I took up one of Scott's novels—*Redgauntlet*', Henry James was later to write, 'it was years since I had read one. They have always a charm for me—but I was amazed at the badness of *R: l'enfance de l'art.*' Amongst writers of prose fiction these two men may well stand as the extremes; and while Scott's heedlessness shocked the author of *A Portrait of a Lady*, Henry James's concern with his art would have seemed to Scott a madman's obsession.

While one reason for Scott's lack of interest in technique was simply the nature of his temperament, and another his pressing need for money, a third may possibly be found in what he believed to have been the practice of Shakespeare. Many English writers are influenced by Shakespeare, and the Shakespeare by whom each is influenced is the Shakespeare presented by the criticism of his day. Whereas modern critics emphasize such matters as Shakespeare's stage-craft and the persistence in his plays of elements originating in the medieval drama, the critics of the late eighteenth and early nineteenth centuries emphasized his spontaneity, contrasting it with the deliberateness of Ben Jonson in terms which sometimes seem to suggest that Jonson's method was that of the non-creative mind, Shakespeare's that of the creator *par excellence*. It is worth remembering this, and the complementary belief that Shakespeare was more concerned with writing fine speeches and creating great characters than with constructing dramatic wholes, when we read Scott's characteristic pronouncements on his own methods of working:

I have repeatedly laid down my future work to scale, divided it into volumes and chapters, and endeavoured to construct a story. . . . But I think there is a demon who seats himself on the feather of my pen when I begin to write, and leads it astray from my purpose. Characters expand under my hand; incidents are multiplied; the story lingers, while the materials increase; my regular mansion turns out a Gothic anomaly. . . . When I light on such a character as Bailie Jarvie, or Dalgetty, my imagination brightens, and my conception becomes clearer at every step which I take in his company. . . . If I resist the temptation . . . my thoughts become prosy, flat and dull . . . I am no more the same author . . . than the dog in a wheel, condemned to go round and round for hours, is like the same dog merrily chasing his own tail.

Introductory Epistle to *The Fortunes of Nigel.*

The magnanimity of this is characteristic of Scott, and thoroughly disarming: he is so frank about his own short-comings that a critic feels embarrassed when he is driven to acknowledge their existence and their importance. Yet there is a hint of complacency underlying the magnanimity. Captain Dalgetty is in a sense the most successful character in *A Legend of Montrose*, but he is quite out of keeping with the general tone of the book and goes far towards turning into farce what had been designed as tragedy. The whole account which Scott gives of his creative processes leads us to expect precisely what we find in the great majority of his tales—ramshackle wholes with magnificent parts.

VI

One of the most remarkable passages in the autobiography is that in which Scott tells us that as a young man he had been passionately anxious to paint landscape. In spite of a great deal of effort, however, he had found himself quite unable 'with the eye of a painter to dissect the various parts

of a scene . . . [or] to assess the effect which various features of
the view had in producing its leading and general effect . . .
Even the humble ambition which I had long cherished of
making sketches of those places which interested me . . .
was totally ineffectual . . . I was obliged to relinquish in
despair an art which I was most anxious to practise.' The
disabilities of men of genius are always of interest, and
Scott's failure as an artist is no less revealing than the lack of
capacity for philosophical discussion which he discovered as
a member of the Speculative Society, or the defective ear
for music which handicapped him as a collector of ballads.
The result seems to have been that while he remained
throughout his life a lover of beautiful scenery, he early
began to specialize (as it were) in scenery with definite
historical associations. He tells us that 'the love of natural
beauty' was one of his fundamental passions, 'more especially
when combined with ancient ruins, or remains of our
fathers' piety or splendour'. 'To me', he says later in the
same passage, 'the wandering over the field of Bannockburn
was the source of more exquisite pleasure than gazing upon
the celebrated landscape from the battlements of Stirling
Castle . . . Show me an old castle or a field of battle, and I
was at home at once, [and] filled it with its combatants in
their proper costume . . . I mention this to show the distinc-
tion between a sense of the picturesque in action and in
scenery.'

Although 'the picturesque in action' is in a sense the clue
to all Scott's books, he did not neglect 'the picturesque . . .
in scenery'. One has only to glance into the various works of
William Gilpin, and particularly his *Observations Relative* . . .
to Picturesque Beauty . . . [*in*] *the High-Lands of Scotland*, to
see how closely many of the scenes that Scott describes
conform to the canons of the picturesque; and when one
finds him praising Mrs Radcliffe for being 'the first to
introduce into her prose fictions a beautiful and fanciful tone
of natural description . . . which had hitherto been
exclusively applied to poetry' it becomes evident that he

regarded picturesque description as one of the resources of the writer of romance. His favourite territory, the Highlands and the Borders, provided him with a rich storehouse of picturesque scenery, and when he moved further afield—to Zetland and Orkney in *The Pirate*, to the Isle of Man in *Peveril of the Peak*—his choice was always partly dictated by the picturesque potentialities of the country. 'The site was singularly picturesque', he remarks at the beginning of *St Ronan's Well*, and it is an observation that might stand at the beginning of the majority of his tales.

Scott's imagination was highly visual and it seems likely that he sometimes conceived of individual episodes, or even whole stories, primarily in visual terms. It is tempting to assign such an origin to *The Bride of Lammermoor*. Near the end of the opening chapter an imaginary painter shows Scott a sketch which contains the germ of the whole book:

The sketch . . . represented an ancient hall, fitted up and furnished in what we now call the taste of Queen Elizabeth's age. The light, admitted from the upper part of a high casement, fell upon a female figure of exquisite beauty, who, in an attitude of speechless horror, appeared to watch the issue of a debate betwixt two other persons. The one was a young man, in the Vandyke dress common to the time of Charles I, who with an air of indignant pride, testified by the manner in which he raised his head and extended his arm, seemed to be urging a claim of right.

The fact that Scott is composing in consciously pictorial terms is often emphasized by his mentioning the name of a particular painter, as he does in this passage. When Ellangowan looks back and sees the gypsies whom he has expelled from their home we are told that 'the group would have been an excellent subject for the pencil of Calotte'. Scott was particularly fond of effects of *chiaroscuro*, and when he uses this device Rembrandt is the painter whom he most often remembers. A fine example is the description of David Deans grieving over the sin of his daughter:

The sun sent its rays through a small window at the old man's back and . . . illumined [his] grey hairs . . . and the sacred page which he studied.

His features, far from handsome, and rather harsh and severe, had yet from their expression of habitual gravity and contempt for earthly things an expression of stoical dignity amidst their sternness . . . The whole formed a picture, of which the lights might have been given by Rembrandt but the outline would have required the force and vigour of Michael Angelo.

Most frequently of all it is his friend David Wilkie whom Scott mentions, as when he says that the scene before the funeral in *The Antiquary* was one 'which our Wilkie alone could have painted, with that exquisite feeling of nature which characterizes his enchanting productions'. The affinity between Fielding and Hogarth has often been pointed out: the affinity between Scott and David Wilkie is no less striking, and no less revealing.

Unlike those of Jane Austen, Scott's finest characters are usually men and women whom we can readily visualize. Edie Ochiltree is a good example, with his 'slouched hat of huge dimensions', his 'long white beard, which mingled with his grizzled hair; an aged but strongly marked and expressive countenance hardened by exposure to a right brick-dust complexion; a long blue gown, with a pewter badge on the right arm; [and] two or three wallets or bags slung across his shoulder'. One notices particularly the explicit contrast between Edie and the Earl:

The contrast . . . was very striking. The hale cheek, firm step, erect stature and undaunted presence and bearing of the old mendicant, indicated patience and content in the extremity of age, and in the lowest condition to which humanity can sink; while the sunken eye, pallid cheek, and tottering form of the nobleman . . . showed how little wealth, power, and even the advantages of youth, have to do with that which gives repose to the mind, and firmness to the frame.

This is only one example of a device to which Scott attached great importance, both in his poems and in his prose romances. Gilpin insists that contrast is an essential element of the picturesque, and one has only to glance through Scott's prefaces to see how often he refers to contrasts of different

kinds. The opening chapter of *Quentin Durward* is headed
'The Contrast', and there are many other chapters which
could bear the same heading. He tells us that he chose a
watering-place as the scene of *St Ronan's Well* because it
is a setting 'where the strongest contrast of humorous
characters and manners may be brought to bear on and
illustrate each other', while in the prefatory letter to *Peveril of
the Peak* he explicitly mentions that once he has found a
suitable subject he 'invests it with such shades of character,
as will best contrast with each other'. This desire for contrast lay very near the heart of Scott's imagination, and
explains part of the appeal that such a character as Rob Roy
had for him. Like Waverley's as he listened to Rose
Bradwardine, Scott's imagination caught fire at the thought
that 'a character like his, blending the wild virtues, the
subtle policy, and unrestrained license of an American
Indian, was flourishing in Scotland during the Augustan
age of Queen Anne and George I'; and he points out in so
many words that it is 'this strong contrast between the
civilized and cultivated mode of life on the one side of the
Highland line, and the wild and lawless adventures . . . [of]
one who dwelt on the opposite side . . . which creates the
interest attached to his name'. It is not surprising that
Scotland in the eighteenth century was for Scott the ideal
imaginative territory. Just as 'the most romantic region of
every country is that where the mountains unite themselves
with the plains or lowlands', so

the most picturesque period of history is that when the ancient rough
and wild manners of a barbarous age are just becoming innovated upon,
and contrasted, by the illumination of increased or revived learning, and
the instructions of renewed or reformed religion. The strong contrast
produced by the opposition of ancient manners to those which are
gradually subduing them, affords the lights and shadows necessary to
give effect to a fictitious narrative; and while such a period entitles the
author to introduce accidents of a marvellous and improbable character,
as arising out of the turbulent independence and ferocity belonging to
old habits of violence, . . . yet . . . the characters and sentiments of many

of the actors may . . . be described with great variety of shading and delineation, which belongs to the newer and more improved period.

Introduction to *The Fortunes of Nigel*.

Scott was never quite certain whether it was a contrast between the enlightened present and the barbarous past or between the prosaic present and the romantic past, and from the heart of this uncertainty he wrote his books.

VII

While there are few writers whose achievement is more difficult to assess, it is clear that Scott's importance is very great. The popularity of his books was prodigious: their circulation exceeded that of the work of any earlier novelist and revolutionized the status of the novel as a vendible commodity. That it has now been the dominant literary form for more than a century is in a considerable measure due to him. Richardson and Fielding had established the novel: Scott made it irresistible. He also confirmed its respectability, which had remained in some doubt throughout the previous century. Few major writers have been so unadventurous in their moral judgements. Once Scott had written it became increasingly difficult for even the strictest of fathers to forbid his daughters to read prose fiction. In this, as in so many other respects, he prepared the way for Dickens. What Dickens did only partially and under restraint, out of deference to the requirements of 'dainty Delicacy', Scott did willingly and from conviction. It is also evident that he extended the range of subject-matter accessible to the novelist. Many writers followed his example in choosing Scottish subjects, while others explored the possibility of dealing with other regions of the British Isles. But his most obvious influence was in popularizing the historical romance. As he himself makes clear in the *Lives of the Novelists*, this type of book was already familiar in the eighteenth century; yet since what matters in literature is not so much being the first to do a thing as being the first to do it outstandingly well and at the critical time, Scott was the important figure. He gave the historical romance a new popularity and a new prestige. He also did something more important. If the nineteenth century was to prove (among other things) the Age of History, the period in which mankind became more conscious of historical perspectives than it had ever been before, it was due to no one more than to Scott. There is abundant evidence of his influence, and the witnesses are the historians themselves. Carlyle is particularly explicit, in an essay which does not err on the side of indulgence:

These Historical Novels have taught all men this truth, which looks like a truism, and yet was as good as unknown to writers of history and others, till so taught; that the bygone ages of the world were actually filled by living men, not by protocols, state-papers, controversies and abstractions of men.

Scott was not a man of ideas, and he shrank from innovation with an instinctive distrust. As Hazlitt put it, 'if you take the universe, and divide it into two parts, he knows all that *has been*; all that *is to be* is nothing to him. . . . The old world is to him a crowded map; the new one a dull, hateful blank.' The paradox is that this man of genius with his gaze fixed on the past did more than most writers have done to change the way in which men and women think and so to create the climate of ideas in which we are still living today.

SIR WALTER SCOTT

A Select Bibliography

(Place of publication London, unless stated otherwise)

Bibliography:

A BIBLIOGRAPHY OF THE WAVERLEY NOVELS, by G. Worthington (1931).

A BIBLIOGRAPHY OF THE POETICAL WORKS, by W. A. Ruff, *Edinburgh Bibliographical Society Transactions*, I, ii–iii (1937-8).

A BIBLIOGRAPHY OF SIR WALTER SCOTT: A CLASSIFIED AND ANNOTATED LIST OF BOOKS AND ARTICLES RELATING TO HIS LIFE AND WORKS, 1797-1940, by J. C. Corson; Edinburgh (1943).

Principal Collected Works:

POETICAL WORKS, 12 vols; Edinburgh (1820).

POETICAL WORKS, ed. J. G. Lockhart, 12 vols; Edinburgh (1833-4).

POETICAL WORKS, ed. J. L. Robertson (1904)
—in the 'Oxford Standard Authors' series.

POETICAL WORKS, ed. L. M. Watt (1942).

MISCELLANEOUS PROSE WORKS, 30 vols; Edinburgh (1834-40; 1871 vols. 29-30)
—these include *The Life of Dryden; Memoirs of Jonathan Swift;* 'Lives of the Novelists'; *Paul's Letters to his Kinsfolk; Border Antiquities;* the essays on *Chivalry* and *Romance; The Life of Napoleon* (9 vols.); numerous reviews (some incorrectly ascribed); and the three series of *Tales of a Grandfather* (7 vols)—all of which had been printed previously.

WAVERLEY NOVELS, 48 vols; Edinburgh (1830-4)
—with Prefaces and Notes by Scott.

Note: Of the many other collected editions of the WAVERLEY NOVELS, mention may be made of the Centenary Edition (text revised, with notes by D. Laing), 25 vols, 1870-1; the Dryburgh Edition, 25 vols, 1892-4; the Border Edition (notes by Andrew Lang), 48 vols, 1892-4; the Edinburgh Edition, 48 vols, 1901-3; the Oxford Scott, 25 vols, 1910. A number of the novels published by Everyman's Library have been re-edited by W. M. Parker, with biographical and bibliographical introductions.

SHORT STORIES, ed. Lord David Cecil (1934)
—in the 'World's Classics' series.

Separate Works:

Note: Scott did not acknowledge the authorship of the WAVERLEY
NOVELS until 1827. *Waverley* was anonymous, while most of its
successors were 'By the author of Waverley'.

THE EVE OF SAINT JOHN: A Border ballad; Kelso (1800)
—Scott had previously published some ballads translated from the
German.

THE LAY OF THE LAST MINSTREL: A Poem (1805).

BALLADS AND LYRICAL PIECES; Edinburgh (1806).

MARMION: A Tale of Flodden Field; Edinburgh (1808). *Verse*

THE LADY OF THE LAKE: A Poem; Edinburgh (1810).

THE VISION OF DON RODERICK: A Poem; Edinburgh (1811).

ROKEBY: A Poem; Edinburgh (1813).

THE BRIDAL OF TRIERMAIN: or, The Vale of St John; Edinburgh (1813).
Verse

WAVERLEY: or, 'Tis Sixty Years since, 3 vols; Edinburgh (1814). *Novel*

GUY MANNERING: or, The Astrologer, 3 vols; Edinburgh (1815). *Novel*

THE LORD OF THE ISLES: A Poem; Edinburgh (1815).

THE FIELD OF WATERLOO: A Poem; Edinburgh (1815).

THE ANTIQUARY, 3 vols; Edinburgh (1816). *Novel*

TALES OF MY LANDLORD, 4 vols; Edinburgh (1816). *Novel*
—contains *The Black Dwarf* and *Old Mortality.* Published under the
pseudonym Jedediah Cleishbotham.

HAROLD THE DAUNTLESS: A Poem; Edinburgh (1817).

ROB ROY, 3 vols; Edinburgh (1818). *Novel*

TALES OF MY LANDLORD. Second series, 4 vols; Edinburgh (1818).
Novel
—contains *The Heart of Mid-Lothian.*

TALES OF MY LANDLORD. Third series, 4 vols; Edinburgh (1819). *Novel*
—contains *The Bride of Lammermoor* and *A Legend of Montrose.*

IVANHOE: A romance, 3 vols; Edinburgh (1820). *Novel*

THE MONASTERY: A romance, 3 vols; Edinburgh (1820). *Novel*

THE ABBOT, 3 vols; Edinburgh (1820). *Novel*

KENILWORTH: A romance, 3 vols; Edinburgh (1821). *Novel*

THE PIRATE, 3 vols; Edinburgh (1822). *Novel*

THE FORTUNES OF NIGEL, 3 vols; Edinburgh (1822). *Novel*

PEVERIL OF THE PEAK, 4 vols; Edinburgh (1822). *Novel*

HALIDON HILL: A Dramatic Sketch from Scottish history; Edinburgh (1822). *Verse*

QUENTIN DURWARD, 3 vols; Edinburgh (1823). *Novel*

ST RONAN'S WELL, 3 vols; Edinburgh (1824). *Novel*

REDGAUNTLET: A Tale of the Eighteenth Century, 3 vols; Edinburgh (1824). *Novel*

TALES OF THE CRUSADERS, 4 vols; Edinburgh (1825). *Novel*
—contains *The Betrothed* and *The Talisman*.

WOODSTOCK: or, The Cavalier. A Tale of the year sixteen hundred and fifty-one, 3 vols; Edinburgh (1826). *Novel*

CHRONICLES OF THE CANONGATE, 2 vols; Edinburgh (1827). *Novel*
—contains *The Highland Widow, The Two Drovers* and *The Surgeon's Daughter*, with an Introduction in which Scott acknowledges his authorship of the Waverley Novels.

CHRONICLES OF THE CANONGATE. Second Series, 3 vols; Edinburgh (1828). *Novel*
—contains *St. Valentine's Day: Or, The Fair Maid of Perth*.

ANNE OF GEIERSTEIN: or, The Maiden of the Mist, 3 vols; Edinburgh (1829). *Novel*

TALES OF MY LANDLORD. Fourth and last series, 4 vols; Edinburgh (1832). *Novel*
—contains *Count Robert of Paris* and *Castle Dangerous*.

THE JOURNAL, 1825-32, ed. D. Douglas, 2 vols; Edinburgh (1890)
—ed. J. G. Tait, 3 vols; Edinburgh, 1939-46.

NEW LOVE-POEMS, ed. D. Cook; Oxford (1932).

Letters:

THE PRIVATE LETTER-BOOKS OF SIR WALTER SCOTT, ed. W. Partington (1930)
—this and the following item contain letters to Scott which are now in the National Library of Scotland.

SIR WALTER'S POST-BAG: More stories and sidelights from his un-published letter-books, ed. W. Partington (1932).

THE LETTERS, ed. Sir H. J. C. Grierson and others, 12 vols. (1932-7)
—an index on cards was prepared by W. M. Parker for the National Library of Scotland, and may be consulted there.

CORRESPONDENCE OF SCOTT AND C. R. MATURIN, ed. F. E. Ratchford and W. H. McCarthy; Austin, Texas (1937).

Note: In addition to a great amount of literary journalism and miscellaneous writing (essays, prefaces, etc.) Scott edited the *Minstrelsy of the Scottish Border*, 2 vols, Kelso, 1802; 3 vols, Edinburgh, 1803; ed. T. F. Henderson, 1902, reissued 1932; the works of Dryden, 18 vols, 1808; the works of Swift, 19 vols, 1814; *Secret History of the Court of James the First*, 2 vols, 1811; and much else besides. His 'Lives of the Novelists' were prefixed to *Ballantyne's Novelist's Library*, 10 vols, 1821-4.

Some Biographical and Critical Studies:

Note: A great deal of criticism is to be found in the reviews of Scott's books which appeared in the *Edinburgh Review*, the *Quarterly*, and other periodicals of the time. Most of the points that have been made by modern critics are anticipated by someone writing in Scott's own day. Some of the best of these reviews—for example, those by Hazlitt and Jeffrey—were reprinted and are mentioned in the list below.

LETTERS TO RICHARD HEBER, ESQ. CONTAINING CRITICAL REMARKS ON THE SERIES OF NOVELS BEGINNING WITH 'WAVERLEY', AND AN ATTEMPT TO ASCERTAIN THEIR AUTHOR [by J. L. Adolphus] (1821)

—an admirable piece of criticism, in which Adolphus shows that *Waverley* and its successors were written by the same man as *Marmion* and the other poems.

THE SPIRIT OF THE AGE; or, Contemporary Portraits [by W. Hazlitt] (1835)

—the 'character' of Scott is one of the most brilliant and incisive criticisms of him ever written. Hazlitt hated Scott's politics, and his essay has a sharp edge. Much else on Scott is to be found in Hazlitt's collected writings.

LIFE OF SIR WALTER SCOTT, BARONET: WITH CRITICAL NOTICES OF HIS WRITINGS, by G. Allan; Edinburgh (1834)

—Corson points out that this appeared in 5 parts between 1832 and 1834, and that the marked difference in tone between the part dealing with Scott's early life and that dealing with his maturity is due to the fact that the first part has been written by a William Weir, not by Allan himself.

THE DOMESTIC MANNERS AND PRIVATE LIFE OF SIR WALTER SCOTT, by J. Hogg; Glasgow (1834)
—by the 'Ettrick Shepherd', who knew Scott very well. Lockhart disliked Hogg, and treats him unfairly.

LIFE OF SIR WALTER SCOTT, by R. Chambers (1834)
—revised and enlarged, 1871.

MEMOIRS OF THE LIFE OF SIR WALTER SCOTT, BART., by J. G. Lockhart, 7 vols; Edinburgh (1837-8)
—most later biographies simply plunder Lockhart, who included Scott's own account of his early life, written in 1808.

CRITICAL AND MISCELLANEOUS ESSAYS, by T. Carlyle, 4 vols (1839).

MODERN PAINTERS, by J. Ruskin, 5 vols (1843; 1846-60)
—Vol. I, 1843; Vol. II, 1846: here and elsewhere—notably in *Fors Clavigera*, *Praeterita* and *Fiction, Fair and Foul*—Ruskin wrote a good deal on Scott and his influence. Some of the most important passages are given by A. H. R. Ball in his useful book of selections, *Ruskin as Lierary Critic*, 1928.

CONTRIBUTIONS TO THE EDINBURGH REVIEW, by F. Jeffrey, 4 vols (1844)
—this and subsequent collections of Jeffrey's criticism contain some of his reviews of *Waverley* and the later books.

'The Waverley Novels', by W. Bagehot, *National Review*, April 1858
—reprinted in his *Works*, and in collections of his essays variously entitled *Literary Studies* and *Estimations in Criticism*.

HOURS IN A LIBRARY, by L. Stephen, 3 series (1874-9)
—the First Series contains an excellent essay on the Waverley Novels.

SIR WALTER SCOTT, by R. H. Hutton (1878)
—in the 'English Men of Letters' series.

THE LITERARY HISTORY OF ENGLAND IN THE END OF THE EIGHTEENTH AND BEGINNING OF THE NINETEENTH CENTURY, by Mrs Oliphant, 3 vols (1882)
—contains a long chapter on Scott which is still of interest.

SIR WALTER SCOTT, by W. H. Hudson (1901).

SIR WALTER SCOTT, by A. Lang (1906).

SIR WALTER SCOTT AND THE BORDER MINSTRELSY, by A. Lang (1910).

THE SCOTT ORIGINALS, by W. S. Crockett (1912)
—an account of the originals of many characters in Scott's work.

COLLECTED ESSAYS OF W. P. KER, ed. C. Whibley, 2 vols (1925)
—Vol. I contains three essays on Scott.

SIR WALTER SCOTT'S CONGÉ, by C. N. Johnston (Lord Sands) (1929)
—deals with Scott's unsuccessful love for Williamina Belsches. It is
essential to consult the third edition of this book, which appeared in
1931, as it was only then that Lord Sands finally settled some very
difficult problems of chronology.

SIR WALTER: a four-part study in biography, by D. Carswell (1930).

SIR WALTER SCOTT, by J. Buchan (1932)
—biographically unoriginal, yet containing perceptive comments on
Scott as a man and an author by another Scottish writer of romances
who understood him very well.

'Scott's . . . use of the supernatural . . . in relation to the chronology
of the Waverley Novels', by M. C. Boatwright, *Publications of
the Modern Language Association of America*, L, March 1935.

THE WAVERLEY NOVELS AND THEIR CRITICS, by J. T. Hillhouse;
Minneapolis (1936).

SCOTT AND SCOTLAND: The predicament of the Scottish writer, by
E. Muir (1936)
—a stimulating book in which the author pointed to the 'very curious
emptiness . . . behind the wealth of his imagination', and tried to
account for it. Muir vividly illustrates the fact that a Scotsman
writing on Scott tends also to be giving his interpretation of the
whole development of Scotland and its culture since the Union of
the Parliaments in 1707. Muir also wrote about Scott in *The English
Novelists: A Survey of the Novel by Twenty Contemporary Novelists*,
ed. D. Verschoyle (1936), as well as in the volume of *Sir Walter
Scott Lectures* mentioned below.

SIR WALTER SCOTT, BART. A NEW LIFE SUPPLEMENTARY TO, AND CORREC-
TIVE OF, LOCKHART'S BIOGRAPHY, by Sir H. J. C. Grierson (1938).

ESSAYS AND ADDRESSES, by Sir H. J. C. Grierson (1940)
—contains 'Scott and Carlyle', and an important essay on 'Lang,
Lockhart and Biography'.

ESSAYS ON THE EIGHTEENTH CENTURY PRESENTED TO DAVID NICHOL
SMITH; Oxford (1945)
—contains an outstanding essay by F. A. Pottle on 'The Power of
Memory in Boswell and Scott'.

SIR WALTER SCOTT, by U. Pope-Hennessy (1948)
—in two parts, 'The Man' and 'The Work'. This brief study makes some interesting critical suggestions, but the theory that some of Scott's novels were written before *Waverley* is irritatingly ubiquitous.

'The chronology of the Waverley Novels: the evidence of the manuscripts', by R. D. Mayo, *Publications of the Modern Language Association of America*, LXIII, September 1948
—argues convincingly against the theory of Dame Una Pope-Hennessy and others. Mayo's view is that the novels were written in the order of publication.

SIR WALTER SCOTT LECTURES, 1940-1948. With an introduction by W. L. Renwick; Edinburgh (1950)
—contains the first four series of Scott Lectures by Sir H. J. C. Grierson, E. Muir, G. M. Young and S. C. Roberts, reprinted from the *University of Edinburgh Journal*, which also contains the subsequent lectures (1950-6) by D. Nichol Smith, J. R. Sutherland, J. C. Corson, M. Lascelles and J. Adam Smith.

LA CRISI DELL'EROE NEL ROMANZO VITTORIANO, by M. Praz; Florence (1952)
—translated by A. Davidson under the title *The Hero in Eclipse in Victorian Fiction*, 1956. Argues that 'the novels of Sir Walter Scott made a notable contribution to the process by which Romanticism turned bourgeois'.

WALTER SCOTT: His life and personality, by H. Pearson (1954).

SCOTTISH POETRY: A critical survey, ed. J. Kinsley (1955)
—contains 'Scottish Poetry in the Earlier Nineteenth Century' by J. W. Oliver.

THE HISTORICAL NOVEL, by G. Lukács; (1962)
—translated by H. and S. Mitchell; a penetrating study, written from a Marxist point of view.

LITERARY ESSAYS, by D. Daiches; Edinburgh (1956)
—'Scott's Achievement as a Novelist' is an admirable appreciation.

REMINISCENCES OF SIR WALTER SCOTT'S RESIDENCE IN ITALY, 1832, by Sir W. Gell, ed. J. C. Corson (1957)
—Lockhart made a rather cavalier use of Gell's reminiscences, and it is interesting to compare the full text with what appears in his *Life*. Gell's *Reminiscences* were also published in Toronto in 1953, edited by G. H. Needler.

THE HEYDAY OF SIR WALTER SCOTT, by D. Davie (1961).

THEY ASKED FOR A PAPER, by C. S. Lewis (1962)
—contains an essay on Scott.

THE HERO OF THE WAVERLEY NOVELS, by A. Welsh; New Haven (1963)
—Yale Studies in English, No. 154.

THE OXFORD HISTORY OF ENGLISH LITERATURE, ed. F. P. Wilson and
B. Dobrée; Oxford (1945-   )
—Vol. IX, *English Literature, 1789-1815*, by W. L. Renwick, 1963,
contains a brief discussion of Scott's poetry; Vol. X, *English
Literature 1815-1832* by Ian Jack, 1963, contains a chapter on 'The
Waverley Romances'.

SCOTT'S NOVELS: The plotting of historic survival, by F. R. Hart;
Charlottesville, Virginia (1966).

THE RUIN OF SIR WALTER SCOTT, by E. Quayle (1968)
—using the Ballantyne papers, Quayle argues that Scott was respon-
sible for his own financial downfall.

THE ACHIEVEMENT OF WALTER SCOTT, by A. O. J. Cockshut (1969).

SIR WALTER SCOTT: The formative years, by A. Melville Clark;
Edinburgh (1969).

TIME, PLACE, AND IDEA: ESSAYS ON THE NOVEL, by J. H. Raleigh;
Carbondale (1968)
—includes a chapter 'What Scott meant to the Victorians'.

IMAGINED WORLDS: ESSAYS . . . IN HONOUR OF JOHN BUTT, ed. M. Mack
and I. Gregor (1968)
—contains 'Scott and the Art of Revision', by M. Lascelles.

SIR WALTER SCOTT ON NOVELISTS AND FICTION, ed. I. Williams (1968)
—a most useful compilation.

SCOTT: The critical heritage, ed. J. O. Hayden (1970)
—a valuable collection of nineteenth-century criticism of Scott.

SIR WALTER SCOTT: The great Unknown, by E. Johnson, 2 vols (1970)
—the most comprehensive biography since Lockhart's: an important
study.

SCOTT'S MIND AND ART, ed. A. Norman Jeffares; Edinburgh (1969)
—ten essays on various aspects of Scott.

THE AUTHOR OF WAVERLEY: A critical study of Walter Scott, by
D. D. Devlin (1971).

LOCKHART AS ROMANTIC BIOGRAPHER, by F. R. Hart; Edinburgh
(1971)
—contains the fullest discussion of Lockhart's biography.

WRITERS AND THEIR WORK